Medieval Monarchs

Nigel Smith

Titles in this series:
Life in Medieval Britain
Medieval Monarchs
The Medieval Church
The Norman Conquest

Cover: William II, part of a stained glass window in Canterbury Cathedral.
Title page: Detail of a manuscript painting showing King John hunting.

Series and book editor:
Geraldine Purcell
Series and book designer:
Simon Borrough
Book consultant:
Dr Matthew Strickland, Lecturer in the Medieval History department of the University of Glasgow

© Copyright 1996 Wayland (Publishers) Ltd

First published in 1996 by Wayland (Publishers) Ltd, 61 Western Road, Hove, East Sussex BN3 1JD

British Library Cataloguing in Publication Data
Smith, Nigel
Medieval Monarchs. - (Medieval Britain)
1. Great Britain - Kings and rulers - Juvenile literature 2. Great Britain - History - Medieval period, 1066-1485 - Juvenile literature
I. Title
942'.00992

ISBN 0 7502 17448

DTP by: Simon Borrough
Printed and bound in Italy by G. Canale & C.S.p.A., Turin.

Picture acknowledgements

Bridgeman Art Library/British Library cover, title page, 13, 15, 17, 18, 19, 23, 29, 30, 32; /Lambeth Palace Library 24, 34-5; Museé Conde 29; Syon House 41; Westminster Abbey 36. C.M. Dixon 6, 8, 43. E.T. Archive 11, 28, 31, 37, 41. Sonia Halliday cover 9, 10. Michael Holford 5 (both). Hulton Deutsch 14. Topham Picture Source 15, 18, 15, 18, 25, 26, 39. Wayland Picture Library 4, /British Museum 16, 22, 33; /National Portrait Gallery 42. Maps on pages 12 and 34 are by Peter Bull.

Contents

Apart from Henry III every medieval king was crowned in a religious ceremony, a coronation, at Westminster Abbey in London.

During the Middle Ages the monarch of England was the most important person in the land. The monarch was widely believed to be God's representative. The coronation ceremony included the anointing of the new ruler with holy oil and was a sacred occasion. Medieval monarchs were all men – there was not a crowned queen of England until Mary I (r.1553–8).

Life for kings was always difficult and surrounded by danger. Often, powerful nobles argued with the king about how much power he should have. Frequently a king had to go into battle and fight to keep his crown and also guard against the schemes of other ambitious men plotting how they could become king. Many medieval kings met a violent death either on the battlefield or as the result of murder and treachery.

The maintenance of peace, law and order was a prime duty which many kings, such as William I, Henry I and Henry II, took very seriously. Although the job of the king was to rule the country, some kings were more interested in power and conquest than in improving the lives of the people. The king had the power of life and death over everyone. Those who angered the king were likely to be executed.

William I

The year 1066 was a very important one in British history. In that year two English kings died and an invader captured the throne.

'By the splendour of God I have taken possession of my realm; the earth of England is in my two hands.'

With those words Duke William of Normandy leapt ashore as he invaded Anglo-Saxon England in September 1066. His forces met the English army led by King Harold at the Battle of Hastings.

After a gruelling fight, King Harold was killed and William became the first Norman king of England. Harold had been king for only ten months. What right had William, who did not even speak English, to be England's king?

William was ambitious and being a king was more important than being a duke. He claimed that the previous English king, Edward the Confessor (r.1042–66), who had grown up in Normandy, had promised that William would be the next king. But, when Edward died in January 1066, it was Earl Harold of Wessex, a powerful and popular Anglo-Saxon noble, who was crowned as the new king. So William invaded England and settled the matter by force.

William I shown in the Bayeux Tapestry. The tapestry was embroidered between 1067 and 1077 and shows the events of the Norman Conquest.

Left *Norman knights leading the attack against Anglo-Saxon foot soldiers at the Battle of Hastings, in another scene from the Bayeux Tapestry.*

Conquering the land

Following his coronation on Christmas Day 1066, at Westminster Abbey, William sent his Norman soldiers to every part of the kingdom. Their task was to establish strongholds by building castles and dealing with anyone who would not accept William as king. At first, William tried to rule with the cooperation of the Anglo-Saxons, but the greed of his Norman nobles for land soon caused bitter resistance.

Although William was a religious man and fair to his friends, he was brutal towards his enemies. When English rebels burnt down a Norman castle at York in 1069, William was furious. He ordered his soldiers to destroy every village, to burn the crops and to kill all the animals over a wide area. This was called the 'harrying of the north' and led to a terrible famine in which many people died from starvation. This is how a monk, Simeon of Durham, described the event:

'It was horrific to see human bodies rotting in the houses and the roads, and there was a terrible smell and a great silence fell over the land.'

The success of William's conquest depended on terror. He built the Tower of London so that he would be safe from attack in his capital city.

Feudalism and homage

William rewarded his Norman supporters by giving them land that he had seized from the English. This helped ensure that they stayed loyal. They shared out some of their land to other Norman soldiers in a system known as feudalism. In return for this land everyone had to promise loyalty and service to the king. This was called homage.

The Conqueror dies

Even as the king of England, William still gave a great deal of attention to his lands in France. In 1087 he attacked a French town whose soldiers had raided his land. He ordered his men to burn down the entire town. As he rode through the burning ruins a hot cinder made his horse stumble. William was thrown off and seriously hurt. He knew he was dying. As he remembered his many cruel deeds, we are told, he became frightened of facing God. On his death bed he is supposed to have said:

'I persecuted the native inhabitants of England beyond all reason, I am stained with the rivers of blood that I have shed.'

The Domesday Book

William needed a constant supply of money to pay for his armies. The king wanted to know all about the people and the land that he ruled. In 1085 he ordered a survey of the country which was completed in 1086. It was later called the Domesday Book, because no one could avoid it, just as no one is supposed to escape doomsday – the last day of the world. In the eleventh century there were fewer than two million people in England. William's officials went to every village to find out how many people lived there, how much land they farmed and how many animals they owned.

'Men were sent into areas which they did not know in order to check the first survey. The land was troubled with much violence from the collection for royal taxes.'

Bishop of Hereford

Compiling the Domesday Book was a great achievement. It records all the information that William needed to know about the state of the country that he had conquered.

This seal was used by William II. Every king had their own seal which was fixed to official documents.

William I had ruled both England and lands in France. When he died his eldest son, Robert, inherited Normandy in France, and another son, William, became the new king of England.

William II

Because of his red face and hair William II (r. 1087–1100) was known as William Rufus. He was a good soldier, well known for his chivalry and generosity to his knights. However, he was quick-tempered and he quarrelled badly with the Church. The Church leaders and monks disapproved of his long hair, which they thought was the sign of a man who drank, gambled and was immoral. In the case of William Rufus they were probably right!

William was a violent man who used brutal force to get his way. In 1088 several Norman barons who were convinced that William's brother, Robert, Duke of Normandy, would be a better king, plotted against William. Faced with rebellion William made all kinds of promises to the native English to win their support. With their help he succeded in smashing the rebellion, but he later broke all the promises. A monk wrote at the time:

'He was harsh and fierce in his rule, and very terrifying. Therefore he was hated.'

This is a picture of William II from the Great West Window at Canterbury Cathedral.

William's death – accident or murder?

William Rufus fought his brother Robert over Normandy and by 1096 he had become Duke. Robert went off to fight in the Crusades. During this time William had also fought another rebellion in England and had made gains in Wales and Scotland. He may not have been a popular king but he was successful. William's great passion, as with most kings and nobles, was hunting. Whilst hunting deer in the New Forest in August 1100 he was killed by an arrow through his heart. The official story was that it was a dreadful accident. But he may have been murdered by his own brother, Henry, who rushed to London to be crowned just four days later. Henry's speed of action led some people to think that he knew his brother was going to die.

At Henry's coronation he promised good government of the kingdom. He quickly married Edith, the sister of King Edgar of Scotland, probably to ensure that he would not be attacked from the north while he concentrated on the danger from the south – from his brother Robert.

In 1101 a violent struggle broke out between Henry (r.1100–35) and Robert, Duke of Normandy, (who had returned from the Crusades) over who should be king. Eventually, in 1106, Henry triumphed. Robert was captured and spent the last twenty-eight years of his life as his brother's prisoner.

Henry I ruled Normandy as well as England and spent a great deal of time there. He was a powerful ruler, who introduced important and popular reforms in the administration of justice.

This stained glass window at Canterbury Cathedral shows Henry I wearing his coronation crown.

Civil war – Stephen and Matilda

Another violent family squabble occurred when Henry died in 1135. Henry's son, William, had drowned in 1120, and so Henry had no male heir. His nephew Stephen was at Boulogne, just a day's sail from England. On hearing the news of Henry's death he dashed to London to be crowned king before Henry's daughter, Matilda, could get there. It was a bold move. But for most of his reign Stephen had to fight off Matilda's attempts to become queen. Although many people thought that a woman could not rule England, her supporters included her uncle, King David of Scotland, who invaded the north, and Robert of Gloucester who raised a rebellion in the West Country. By 1139 there were two rival courts in England, although Stephen was in the better position. Matilda's best chance for the throne came in 1141–2. When her campaign failed in 1148 she left the country.

This picture shows King Stephen holding a church (representing Christianity). It is part of an illustration of four Norman Kings, William I, William II, Henry I and Stephen.

Henry IIs dominions in 1154

Stephen had prepared his own son Eustace to be king but when Eustace died in 1153, Stephen was persuaded that he should adopt Matilda's son, Henry, and name him heir to the throne. When Stephen died in October 1154, Henry Plantagenet (r.1154–89) became the first medieval king not to be challenged for the throne. Henry II's empire was said to stretch 'from the Arctic Ocean to the Pyrenees'. He was lord of Normandy (from his grandfather) and Anjou (from his father); also through his wife, Eleanor of Aquitaine, he ruled southern France. Henry had enormous energy and was a powerful and respected ruler.

Henry and the murder of Becket

Henry frequently quarrelled with the Church. In 1162 he appointed a friend of his, Thomas Becket, Archbishop of Canterbury (the highest office in the Christian Church in England) in the hope that this would stop the disagreements. But Becket took his responsibility very seriously. He said that the king must not interfere in Church matters. Henry angrily called Becket a traitor. For five years Becket lived abroad before the quarrel was patched up. But, after his return, Becket continued to defy the king. In anger Henry shouted, *'Will no one rid me of this turbulent priest?'* On hearing those words four knights decided to kill Becket. They travelled to Canterbury and tried to drag the archbishop out of his cathedral. Becket clung to a pillar. So they killed him there with several blows to his head. Becket is supposed to have cried out:

> *'I am ready to die for my Lord, that in my blood the Church may obtain liberty and peace.'*

Henry was appalled by the murder. Although he was angry with Becket he knew that it was a terrible thing for the Archbishop of Canterbury to be killed in his own cathedral. People believed that Becket had died for his faith and the Pope, the head of the Christian Church, declared he was a saint. Pilgrims went to pray at the spot where he was killed. Henry went there to pray for forgiveness. Even so the king was better off with Becket out of the way.

Too many sons

Henry and Eleanor had had eight children including Henry, Richard, Geoffrey and John. Henry II took the unusual step of having his son, Henry, crowned in his own lifetime as 'the Young King', in 1170. Henry II did this in the hope of avoiding civil war when he died. But the king's final years were spoilt by his four sons rebelling against him. He travelled throughout England and France, trying to keep the nobles and soldiers loyal to him. In 1183, Young Henry died, as did Geoffrey in 1186. Richard made a treaty with the new king of France and invaded England in 1189, joined by John. In the end Henry died exhausted and heartbroken at the treachery of his children.

Henry II is remembered mainly for the dreadful murder of Archbishop Becket. But he was important as a 'law-giver'. He greatly improved the legal system, including trials by jury, and was concerned that there should be a proper system of law and order throughout his kingdom.

Richard I – the 'Lionheart'

This nineteenth-century statue of Richard I stands outside the Houses of Parliament in London.

Two of Henry II's sons became king in turn. Firstly, Richard I who captured peoples' imagination and is remembered as a hero. However his brother John, who followed Richard as king, is said to have been possibly the worst English king.

Richard was crowned after the death of his father in 1189 and he reigned for ten years. But he actually spent only seven months of that time in England. Richard was more French than English; he had grown up in France and could not speak English. So, it is not surprising that even when he was king of England he preferred to live in lands he ruled in France. Richard was a great soldier and enjoyed going to war. It was his courage in battle that his subjects admired and earned him the title, 'Lionheart'. He was also religious and worried about his various sins, so he was pleased when the opportunity came to fight in a war that he thought would please God – the Crusades.

Crusade – a holy war?

The Crusades were wars to bring the Holy Land under Christian control. The Pope, as head of the Church, called on Christian kings to drive out the Muslims who occupied the land where Jesus Christ had lived.

Richard decided to lead the Third Crusade to free Jerusalem from the control of the powerful Muslim leader, Saladin.

After his coronation Richard stayed in England only long enough to raise money to pay for the Crusade. He sold everything he could, including castles and towns, and even said:

'I would sell London if I could find anyone rich enough to buy it.'

When Richard set off in 1189 it was to be four years before he set foot in England again. He achieved remarkable success against Saladin but failed in his real goal of capturing the important holy city of Jerusalem.

This manuscript illustration shows Richard's coronation

Richard held hostage

On his way home from the Holy Land Richard was first of all shipwrecked and then held prisoner in Austria, where the ruler 'sold' him to the German Emperor. During Richard's absence from England his brother, John, tried to usurp (capture) the throne, in 1193. the attempt failed and Queen Eleanor acted as regent until Richard's return. In 1194, after over a year in prison, Richard was freed in return for a huge ransom. He then made a three-month visit to England. For the next five years Richard remained in France, fighting to regain lands that had been lost whilst he had been held captive.

The Lionheart's last roar

Richard's great enemy Saladin, the Sultan of Egypt and Syria and the leader of the Muslim forces, had once complimented him as a fine soldier:

> *'your king is a man of honour and very brave ... he plunges into the midst of danger.'*

Richard was brave but he risked his life in battle once too often. In 1199, during an attack on a small French castle defended by only fifteen soldiers, he foolishly rode out into the open without armour and was hit by a bolt fired from a crossbow. At the age of only forty-one Richard the Lionheart was dead.

Fighting in the Crusades was vicious and cruel. This picture shows Christians being attacked by Muslims.

A manuscript painting showing King John hunting a stag.

People did not trust the new king, John, because he had been disloyal to Richard. He was very different from his brother. Perhaps John was unlucky to have followed such a popular and heroic king. Richard once said of him:

'My brother John is not the man to conquer a country if there is anyone to offer even the feeblest resistance.'

John had none of Richard's military skill or courage. Before long he had lost most of the lands in France that his brother had ruled. When he failed to win them back he was called 'Soft-sword'. People complained about his defeats and the high taxes they paid for his expensive wars with France. When John left his wife, Isabella of Gloucester, to marry a fourteen-year–old French heiress, it led the King of France to seize Normandy. English nobles were furious with John because they had owned land in Normandy.

The Magna Carta

The Magna Carta was supposed to stop the king ignoring the wishes of the barons and the Church. For the first time a limit was put on the power of the king. These were some of the important points the king was supposed to accept:

- No one was to be put in prison without a proper trial
- The taxes paid to the king had to be fair
- The king was not to interfere with the Church
- No one was to have their property seized by the king.

The Magna Carta meant that even a king had to obey the law and to consult other important people in the kingdom.

This picture, painted in the 19th century, shows King John signing the Magna Carta, surrounded by his barons.

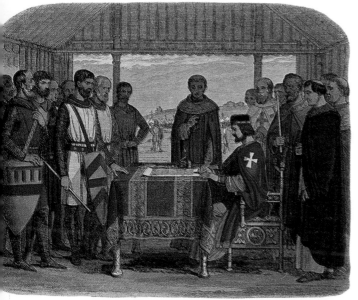

John and the Magna Carta

In the Middle Ages the only form of government was rule by the king alone, sometimes with an advisory council. The barons were fed up with John's high taxes and defeats in battle. They rebelled and captured London in May 1215 and they drew up a list of grievances. The rebel barons warned John that he should consult them and they insisted that he sign a document to that effect.

On 15 June 1215 in a meadow at Runnymede, near the River Thames, John reluctantly signed the document. This was later called the Magna Carta, or Great Charter. John knew that if he refused, a civil war would break out between himself and the barons.

Soon after signing, John announced that he would not after all obey Magna Carta. He tried to punish the barons who had forced him to sign it, but the barons would not give in without a fight. It seemed that England would have to suffer a long and bitter civil war, and the rebel barons even invited Louis, the son of the king of France, to be their ruler. But, when John died in the following year, 1216, there was no reason for the war to continue.

The reign of Henry III (r.1216–72) lasted for fifty-six years. Many changes occurred during his reign.

John's son, Henry, was only nine years old when he became king and he was obviously too young to take important decisions and govern the country. So a regent was appointed to rule until Henry was old enough. During this period and upon Henry's coronation the terms of Magna Carta were in operation.

At the age of twenty Henry began ruling the country, but it was soon clear that he had little talent for governing properly. He was extremely extravagant and unsuccessful in war. Before long Henry had disregarded his earlier promise to follow Magna Carta and had saddled himself with enormous debts, which he tried to pay by demanding more and more money from the barons.

Henry III being crowned by two bishops.

De Montfort – king in all but name

One baron, Simon de Montfort, was a great problem to Henry III. De Montfort was originally from the French court but came to England to become Earl of Leicester and had married Henry's sister, Eleanor. The barons chose de Montfort to lead their revolt against the king. They were increasingly angry over the way Henry ruled the country and for following the bad advice of French advisors.

De Montfort referred back to the Magna Carta and said that the king had to listen to the nobles and could not do whatever he liked. De Montfort forced Henry to accept a set of rules, called the Provisions of Oxford. When Henry went back on his word a civil war broke out in 1264. At the battle of Lewes, de Montfort captured Henry and his son, Prince Edward, and kept them in prison.

This picture shows the death of Simon de Montfort.

The birth of Parliament

For more than a year de Montfort ruled England in the name of the king and called assemblies that were becoming known as 'parliaments'. Some historians regard de Montfort as 'the father of the House of Commons' because he summoned some of the important citizens, called commoners, from each town as well as the nobles. But one of the reasons Henry was unpopular was because he had let himself be influenced by foreigners. Those opposed to de Montfort pointed out that now England's government was in the hands of a Frenchman, de Montfort himself.

Prince Edward escaped from prison in 1264. He was supported by royalists and also gained support from other nobles by promising to reform the role of king. He organized an army and at the battle of Evesham, de Montfort was killed and Henry III was able to rule again.

Royal support of Parliament

When Edward became king after his father's death in 1272 he remembered his promise made in 1264 for reform and he actually continued with de Montfort's idea of Parliament. In 1295 he summoned a Parliament of both the Lords and Commons. This has been called the 'Model Parliament' because it confirmed the idea that Parliament should play an important part in governing the country. Edward accepted that he should not make people pay taxes unless Parliament agreed that they were fair and necessary.

It was a very important step for the king to make this agreement.

It is also important to remember that the ordinary people, the peasants, who made up ninety-five per cent of the population, had no say in Parliament. Even so the need for a king to obtain the agreement of others before he could change taxes certainly reduced his power. Without money a king could not raise an army or go to war.

Edward I was very concerned with the law. He was also interested in all the different groups of people in England. In this picture he is meeting monks and bishops.

'And we have granted, for us and our heirs, that we will not take any taxes from our realm without the consent of all the realm.'

Edward 1, 1297

Alexander Rex Scotore

Lewellin princeps wallie

Edward I in Parliament. The King's officials are sitting on the woolsacks while bishops and noble men sit on the side benches.

The conquest of Wales

Edward was determined to rule both Wales and Scotland as well as England. In 1282 his armies defeated and killed the courageous Welsh leader, Llewelyn ap Gruffydd (whose title was Prince of Wales). The Welsh hated the loss of their freedom. The Snowdonian Mountains, Llewelyn's former power base, were ringed by castles built by Edward to secure the region for the English. These castles were a constant reminder of the influence of England in Wales. To try and please the Welsh Edward made his son, the future Edward II, the new Prince of Wales. But the Welsh still regarded Llewelyn as a hero for trying to stop the English takeover of Wales.

The victorious Scots

Although he was known as the 'Hammer of the Scots' Edward failed to conquer Scotland. In 1296, he invaded the country and said that there would be no more kings of Scotland. Instead the king of England would also be the king of Scotland. Scottish kings had always been crowned sitting on a special stone at Scone Abbey, near Perth. The Stone of Scone was seized and placed under the English coronation chair in Westminster Abbey, in London. When the Scots resisted Edward he twice led his armies to defcat the rebels.

Robert Bruce and his first wife in 1306 when he was secretly crowned King of Scotland (see next page). Edward deported Bruce's wife and hanged his brothers but he could not defeat Bruce.

After a number of successful battles against the English the heroic Scottish leader, William Wallace, was captured and tortured to death in 1305.

But the Scots did not give up their fight for independence. In 1306 Robert Bruce was secretly crowned as King of Scotland. Edward I, at the age of sixty-eight, led an army to meet Robert Bruce's forces, but in July 1307 the English king died before reaching the Scottish border.

The Siege of Berwick in 1297. Edward I failed in his efforts to control the Scots and make them accept him as their king.

This manuscript illustration shows Edward II on his throne.

A divided kingdom

The old king left his son, Edward II, with debts of more than £60,000, which in the fourteenth century was a huge sum. The arguments continued over just how much power the king should have. At first Edward II had the friendship and support of most nobles. But his foolish and stubborn behaviour gradually turned them against him.

Many nobles deeply disliked the king's closest friend and advisor, Piers Gaveston. They refused to meet the king if Gaveston was present. Finally they presented the king with a list of their complaints. A committee, called the Lords' Ordainers, insisted that Gaveston be exiled to live abroad. In future, they demanded, the king must obtain the agreement of Parliament before he appointed anyone to an important position. Edward was told that Parliament would meet twice a year whether the king wanted it to or not.

Although these demands, called Ordinances, contained many good ideas for improving the government of the country, Edward hated them.

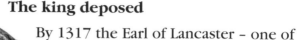

Edwar II's seal.

People welcomed Edward's downfall and agreed when the Archbishop of Canterbury said:

'The king is incompetent to govern in person. Throughout his reign he has been controlled and governed by others who have given him evil counsel.'

John de Stratford, Archbishop of Canterbury, 1327.

The king deposed

By 1317 the Earl of Lancaster – one of the richest and most powerful nobles – had control of the country and Edward was a mere 'puppet king'. But, after 1322, Edward gained royalist support and when he confronted Lancaster, the earl made the mistake of asking Robert Bruce for help. The northern English nobles hated Lancaster for this treachery and defeated him at the Battle of Boroughbridge. Edward was king again, but not for long.

It was Edward's own wife, Queen Isabella, who eventually deposed him. Born in France, people called Isabella the 'She-Wolf of France'. Isabella was an independent woman and she became the lover of Roger Mortimer, one of Edward's most dangerous enemies. Mortimer had been imprisoned by the king in the Tower of London. He managed to escape and, with Isabella, assembled an army and captured Edward in 1326. Edward was forced to give up his crown and take the title, 'Lord Edward sometime King of England'.

But it was not enough for Edward's enemies that he was no longer king. A little while later he was murdered whilst being held prisoner at Berkeley Castle in Gloucestershire.

The new king, Edward III, was only fourteen years old when he was crowned in 1327, so his mother, Isabella, and Mortimer ruled in his place. But in 1330 Edward showed quite firmly that he was taking charge by having Mortimer executed and his mother made a virtual prisoner.

A glorious king

In the Middle Ages, kings were expected to be good soldiers and to lead their armies to victory. In this Edward III was very successful. His reign saw the start of the long struggle between England and France known as the Hundred Years' War. It was actually a series of wars. The main cause was the claim by English kings to the French throne. After the French lost two great naval battles Parliament declared Edward to be 'King of the Sea'.

At first Edward III's many victories at the start of the Hundred Years' War made him very popular.

27

English longbow archers were victorious at the Battle of Crécy in 1346. When they ran out of arrows they simply pulled them out of dead bodies and used them again.

In France Edward III and his son, Edward the Black Prince, led his armies to two victories at the battles of Crécy and Poitiers. King Edward was admired as the greatest warrior in western Europe.

The Black Death

In 1348 a dreadful illness called plague, which had spread across Europe, reached England. As many as one million people, about a third of the population, died from the disease, known as 'the Black Death'.

The king issued these orders to the Lord Mayor of London:
'You are to make sure that all the human excrement and other filth lying in the streets is removed. You are to make sure that there are no more bad smells for people to die from.'

The Black Death caused a shortage of labour. Wages went up and by the end of Edward III's reign the position of the peasant workers was much stronger.

This picture shows a religious procession to end a plague in Rome. During the Middle Ages people believed that prayer could save them from disease and disaster.

Edward III's eldest son, known as the Black Prince, died before his father. The succession to the throne passed to the Black Prince's son Richard and not to King Edward's other son, John of Gaunt. When Edward died in 1377, Richard became king – he was ten years old.

The young King Richard II meeting his officials and noblemen at his Court shortly after his coronation in 1377. They are promising loyalty to their new King.

The Peasants' Revolt

The peasants wanted more freedom and higher wages. Their anger boiled over in 1381 when everyone was ordered to pay a tax called the poll tax. People left their fields and villages and, led by Wat Tyler and John Ball, marched on London. This was called the Peasants' Revolt and nothing like it had happened before. It is believed that as many as 60,000 took part. They set fire to the homes of the nobles, threw open the prisons, murdered the Archbishop of Canterbury and even broke into the Tower of London. It seemed that King Richard was in great danger.

Although he was only fourteen years old Richard showed great bravery, as well as cunning. He rode out to face the rebels. One of the king's supporters killed the rebel leader Wat Tyler and it seemed that the crowd would attack the king. But Richard met the crisis by riding forward alone and telling the crowd: *'I will be your leader. You shall have all you seek.'*

The plight of the peasants

Most English people were poor peasants. They worked on the land struggling to produce enough food for themselves and to pay their taxes to the lords who owned the land. They often went hungry. William Langland, a fourteenth century writer, described the unfair differences between the lives of the rich and poor in his famous poem *Piers Plowman*:

'Some laboured at plowing and sowing, with no time for pleasure, sweating to produce food for the gluttons to waste.
Others spent their lives in vanity, parading them selves in a show of fine clothes.'
Piers Plowman by William Langland, 1370.

Wat Tyler, the rebel leader, was killed by one of Richard's supporters.

Richard's action did the trick. It brought the revolt to an end. He promised to accept the peasant's demands. The young king also promised that nobody would be punished as long as they returned to their homes. But Richard did not keep his word. As soon as it was all over Richard sent his soldiers to round up the rebel leaders and execute them. He told them: *'You are not worthy to live when compared with the lords whom you have attacked.'*

Although the revolt was broken, gradually the peasants' lives improved. As the peasants had discovered, Richard was a strong and ruthless ruler. When he was older he demanded complete obedience from everyone including the nobles. He never forgave anyone who opposed him. People called him a tyrant. He thought he could rule without consulting Parliament.

Richard's use of violence and terror turned many people against him so that in September 1399 he was forced to give up his Crown.

Henry and the House of Lancaster's rise to the throne

Henry Bolingbroke, the son of John of Gaunt and so Richard's cousin, decided that the king should be removed. Bolingbroke had earlier been exiled and in 1399 his father's lands were taken by the king – even though John of Gaunt, as the head of the House of Lancaster (see page 37), had been loyal to Richard. Henry soon had the support of others who disliked the king. Richard was forced to give up the crown to Bolingbroke. A year later Richard died in mysterious circumstances in Pontefract Castle. The official story was that he starved himself to death. Some people claimed that he was suffocated.

The Rise of the House of Lancaster

Henry Bolingbroke's right to be the king may have been doubted by many people, but many others, including Parliament, welcomed him. Henry thought of himself as having been elected, or chosen, as king. Unlike Richard, Henry knew that the powers of a king were limited. Parliament had more say in how money was raised in taxes and how the king spent it. Every year the king's officials gave Parliament detailed accounts. Nothing like this had ever been allowed by a king before.

A troubled reign

Henry IV's reign was disappointing. People had many problems which he was quite powerless to solve. Several bad harvests brought great misery and hardship to the poor. England's main industry, the making of woollen cloth, suffered a serious fall in sales.

Crime increased as bands of poor people roamed the countryside.

Henry also had to deal with rebellions in Wales and Scotland. The Welsh had a strong leader in Owain Glyndwr, who carried on a brave struggle against English rule. Henry IV sent his son, Henry, to finally defeat the Welsh at Harlech in 1409.

Although Henry Bolingbroke may not have been entitled to be King, he was popular when he was crowned in 1399.

The last years

Henry IV was in poor health for the last years of his reign. He also had serious quarrels with his son, Henry, which were only forgiven on the king's death bed. Henry IV died at Westminster Palace in 1413. At the age of only forty-seven he was worn out.

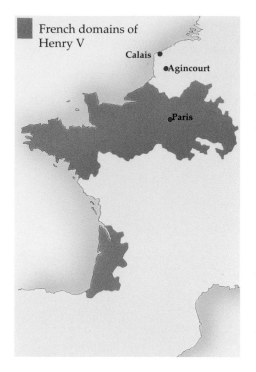

French domains of Henry V

Calais

Agincourt

Paris

Henry V ruled for only nine years (1413–22) and died at the age of thirty-five. Yet he stands out as one of the greatest medieval kings. This is mainly because of his famous victory over the French at the Battle of Agincourt. The playwright, William Shakespeare, wrote one of his most popular plays about Henry V, which helped to ensure his fame and reputation as a great king. However some historians think that Henry was actually wrong to go to war again with France. Henry wanted England to rule France but there was really no chance of success.

Wars with France

The Hundred Years' War had begun in Edward III's reign and continued on and off through the reigns of several kings. Not long after becoming king, Henry took up the English claim to the French throne. He demanded that the French should hand back land which had been ruled by the kings of England 200 years earlier – including Normandy, Maine and Aquitaine, the lands lost by King John. It was an outrageous demand. But the English supported their king and the idea of war with France was popular. It suited Henry to unite all the people of England against an enemy.

The Battle of Agincourt

Henry was certainly a brave and popular leader. But his reputation rests mainly on what happened on a single day, the 25 October 1415, in the countryside of northern France. By then sickness and wounds from earlier battles had reduced Henry's army to about five thousand soldiers. At Agincourt they faced a very confident French army of over twenty thousand soldiers. Against these overwhelming odds the English seemed doomed to defeat and certain death. Henry tried to reach an agreement with the French but they were keen to fight and destroy the English army. Henry never showed any doubt in front of his men. He told them they were God's people and,

'He has entrusted them to me today and He can bring down the pride of these Frenchmen who boast of their numbers and strength.'

King Henry V, before the Battle of Agincourt

At the start of the battle the English soldiers kissed the ground as a kind of prayer to

The battlefield of Agincourt. Henry's great victory made him the most important ruler in Europe.

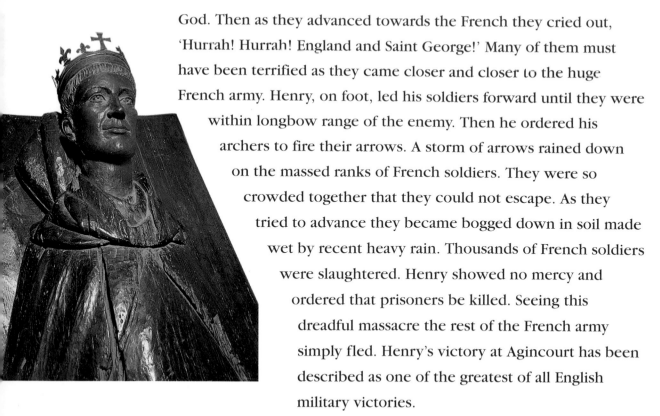

God. Then as they advanced towards the French they cried out, 'Hurrah! Hurrah! England and Saint George!' Many of them must have been terrified as they came closer and closer to the huge French army. Henry, on foot, led his soldiers forward until they were within longbow range of the enemy. Then he ordered his archers to fire their arrows. A storm of arrows rained down on the massed ranks of French soldiers. They were so crowded together that they could not escape. As they tried to advance they became bogged down in soil made wet by recent heavy rain. Thousands of French soldiers were slaughtered. Henry showed no mercy and ordered that prisoners be killed. Seeing this dreadful massacre the rest of the French army simply fled. Henry's victory at Agincourt has been described as one of the greatest of all English military victories.

The tomb of Henry V at Westminster Abbey.

The trouble was that in spite of this one major victory it did not settle the matter of who was going to rule France. In the long run there was no chance that England would ever completely defeat the French. But the amazing victory helped make Henry the most popular king England had ever had. The returning soldiers with their tales of bravery and victory made certain that everyone knew what had happened at Agincourt.

Alliances and absences

Henry married the King of France's daughter, Princess Catherine, in 1420, but this alliance did not end the battles in France. At the time of his death in 1422, Henry the Conqueror, as he was sometimes called, was still fighting in France. His exciting life had been a short one. On his death his brother John declared:

'King Henry the Fifth, too famous to live long!'

Henry VI: the Wars of the Roses

enry VI became king as an infant. His mother, Catherine, was now married again, to a powerful noble called Owen Tudor. The boy-king was raised at court by a Protector and Council. During this time the situation in France went badly and there was much squabbling at the court. Even when he gained his minority in 1437 the king did not have much control.

The Wars of the Roses

During the fifteenth century there was a great struggle between two powerful families over who should be the king. Henry VI, from the House of Lancaster, had none of the skill or bravery of his father, Henry V. Many people thought that Richard, the Duke of York, would make a better king. This argument over the throne led to the Wars of the Roses. Henry and his House of Lancaster used a white rose as their emblem; Richard, and the House of York, used a red rose symbol.

The long reign of Henry VI was disastrous and divided the English people against one another in a civil war.

If Henry VI had been a better king then Richard of York would probably not have opposed him. But Henry was hopeless at war and quite unable to rule the country properly. By 1453 England had lost all the lands they had once ruled in France apart from the town of Calais. Defeat in France brought disgrace upon Henry.

At that time all the important families kept their own private armies. Many of the soldiers returning from France joined them. During the Wars of the Roses these armies were used to fight for or against the king. The wars divided the English people. The Yorkists had the support of nearly all the wealthy families in the southern part of England. Those in the north usually sided with the Lancastrians.

In the first battle of St Albans in 1455 King Henry's army was defeated by the Yorkists. But even after he had won, Richard of York said that he did not want to be king. His intention, he said, was to make sure that England was governed properly when the king was ill. Richard was twice appointed Protector to take over from the king when he was too sick to govern.

However, Henry's queen, Margaret, resented Richard having any power at all. If the king could not govern then Margaret thought that she should do so. Henry, sick and feeble, was anxious to avoid any more bloodshed but Margaret was determined to destroy the Yorkists. In the summer of 1460 the war between the two sides became deadly serious. At the Battle of Wakefield the Lancastrians completely defeated the Yorkists and Richard was killed.

Victory for the House of York

Under the command of the Earl of Warwick, the Yorkists were determined to get revenge for Richard's death. They succeeded at the terrible Battle of Towton. It was the bloodiest battle of the Wars of the Roses, and probably the bloodiest ever fought on English soil. The fighting took place in a blinding snow-storm. This time the Lancastrians were completely beaten. As they tried to escape from the battlefield wearing their heavy armour many of them fell in the River Towton and drowned. Others were deliberately killed even after they had surrendered. We do not know for sure but it is thought as many as 40,000 soldiers died.

For the time being the wars were over. The victorious Yorkists made Richard's son, Edward, the new king (Edward IV). Queen Margaret and her son escaped abroad. Henry VI (now old) was taken prisoner. He was paraded through the streets of London and imprisoned in the Tower of London.

King Edward IV was popular. He did not give people any more freedom and he ignored Parliament, but people were happy that there was peace and that their new king had no need to charge them high taxes to pay for wars.

The wars continue

In fact the Wars of the Roses were not entirely over. So long as Henry remained alive those who supported the Lancastrian cause wanted to make him king again. Their chance came when, after a few years, Edward IV fell out with the powerful Earl of Warwick who had helped him become king. Warwick, called the 'King-maker', was furious with Edward and set Henry free from the Tower of London and made him king again. Edward fled to Holland.

This picture shows Edward IV surrounded by courtiers.

A few months later Edward returned and marched with an army on London. Just outside the city the two sides met at the Battle of Barnet. It was Easter Sunday 1471. In thick mist, Warwick was accidently killed by his own men and the victorious Edward once again became king. Henry was sent back to the Tower of London where he died soon after. There is little doubt that Edward IV ordered his murder. Henry's only son was killed in battle. With their deaths Edward's position was secure and he ruled for a further twelve years.

Edward IV's secret marriage

When a king married it was usually to unite two important families and perhaps increase the amount of land they owned. Edward's advisors wanted him to marry the sister of the French queen, to help keep peace between England and France. To everyone's amazement, just as the arrangements for the marriage were nearly completed, the king admitted that he was already married. It came as a shock that the king had secretly married a widow from a family that had supported his enemies, the Lancastrians.

Richard III was quite ruthless in achieving his ambition to be King. some historians see him as a 'bloodstained monster'.

Richard and the two princes

When Edward IV died in 1483 he left two sons, Edward V aged thirteen and Richard aged eleven. The dying king had chosen his brother, Richard of Gloucester, to rule as Protector until Edward was old enough to be king. Edward made a great mistake in giving this power to his brother. Richard was ambitious and determined to be king himself. Many of the leading men from King Edward's reign were arrested and executed. Edward's two young sons were placed in the Tower of London. Richard said it was for their own protection. They were never seen again. No one is quite sure what happened to them but they were almost certainly murdered on the orders of their uncle. If Richard was guilty then it was a terrible crime. But Richard had succeeded in becoming king.

The rule of Richard III

No one trusted Richard III and he was always afraid that someone would try to take the throne away from him. He wanted his son to follow him as king. When his young son died after a short illness it was a terrible shock. At the time a nun wrote:

'this only son of his, in whom all the hopes of the royal succession were centred ...You might have seen his father and mother in a state almost bordering on madness, by reason of their sudden grief.'

Croyland Chronicle.

The threat of Henry Tudor

Many of the nobles that Richard had relied on began to turn against him. They supported Henry Tudor, the last of the Lancastrians. Henry raised an army and fought Richard at the Battle of Bosworth, in 1485. Richard was not a coward — he died fighting on the battlefield. It was the last time an English king was killed in battle. Richard had been king for only two years and two months. His crown was picked out of a bush and placed on the head of Henry Tudor. In 1486 Henry married Elizabeth of York, Edward IV's daughter, giving him an even stronger reason for taking the throne.

The brutal struggle of the Wars of the Roses was finally over. Historians have traditionally seen this point as the end of the Middle Ages, though some would argue that the process was a more gradual change over the reigns of Henry VII and Henry VIII.

This coin was minted to commemorate Henry's marriage to Elizabeth of York in 1486. Their marriage helped bring together the Lancastrians and the Yorkists and bring about peace between the warring families.

Henry VII (r. 1485–1509) was the first king from the Tudor family. Tudor kings and queens ruled for the next 118 years.

Henry had become king by winning the Battle of Bosworth. He worried that someone might try to take the crown from him by force. But so many nobles had been killed off during the Wars of the Roses that there was no one left to oppose him.

It had been a clever move for Henry to make peace with his old enemy, the House of York, by marrying Elizabeth, the daughter of Edward IV. To reduce the power of the nobles even further, Henry made it illegal to keep a private army.

Henry VII as king

Any noble who disobeyed him was taken to the Court of Star

Henry VII brought peace and security to England.

Chamber, so called because of the stars painted on the ceiling of the room where it met. The Court gave the defendants the choice of paying a huge fine or being imprisoned in the Tower of London. Henry wanted them to pay the fines because he wanted their money – fines could be the equivalent of £1 million today. To raise more money he 'sold' important jobs. Henry used the money to employ more soldiers so that he would be safe and powerful.

Although Henry was not a popular king the country was glad that there was peace at home and abroad. The wealthy merchants and gentlemen who owned land were glad that they could get on with making more money for themselves. Henry kept on good terms with other European countries which was quite unusual for an English king. This helped the important cloth trade. But the strain and worry of being king damaged his health. An ambassador who met Henry VII wrote of him:

> *'Young for his years but old for the sorrowful life he has led.'*

Still worrying that he would lose his throne, he died at the age of fifty-two.

Medieval monarchy ended when Henry VIII became king in 1509 and started a new era in British History.

The legacy of Henry Tudor

Henry left his son, who became Henry VIII, with a strong and respected monarchy. There was a proper system of law and order. The government was efficient and he left a large fortune for his son. But Henry VII had governed without Parliament. The arguments over how much power a king should have and the role of Parliament in governing the country were going to cause great problems in the future. In time Parliament became more important than the monarch. Today, the monarch has no real power. Medieval monarchs would not have understood or liked our system of parliamentary democracy.

Timeline

Saxon

1066	Harold II
	Battle of Hastings

House of Normandy

1066-87	**William I (the Conqueror)**
1085–6	Domesday Survey
1087-1100	**William II (Rufus)**
1100-35	Henry I

House of Blois

1135-54	Stephen
1139–53	civil war in England – Stephen and Matilda

House of Plantagenet

1154-89	Henry II
1169	English conquest of Ireland began
1170	Murder of Thomas Becket in Canterbury Cathedral
1189-99	**Richard I (the Lionheart)**
1190–92	King Richard I led the Third Crusade
1199-1216	John
1215	King John signed the Magna Carta; civil war in England
1216-72	**Henry III**
1265–5	government of Simon de Montfort
1272-1307	**Edward I**
1282–3	Edward I conquered Wales
1295	the 'Model Parliament'
1296	Edward I invaded Scotland
1306	Scottish rebellion of Robert Bruce
1307-27	**Edward II**
1321–2	civil war in England

1327-77	Edward III
1337	start of the Hundred Years' War
1348	the Black Death
1377-99	Richard II
1381	the Peasants' Revolt
1387	Geoffrey Chaucer started writing *The Canterbury Tales*

House of Lancaster

1399-1413	Henry IV
1400–10	rebellion of Owain Glyndwr in Wales
1413-22	Henry V
1415	battle of Agincourt
1422-71	Henry VI
1453	end of the Hundred Years' war
1455	start of the Wars of the Roses

House of York

1471-83	Edward IV
1476	William Caxton set up the first printing press in England
1483	Edward V
1483-5	Richard III
1485	end of the Wars of the Roses

House of Tudor

1485-1509	Henry VII
1492	Christopher Columbus made his first crossing of the Atlantic Ocean
1509	death of Henry VII. Some historians say the Middle Ages ended 1485 or at least by 1509.

Ambassador The representative of a government in another country.

Anglo-Saxon The name given to the people living in England before the Norman Conquest.

Annointing Applying oil to a person as part of a religious ceremony.

Chivalry Bravery and courtesy shown by medieval knights and nobles.

Christian Someone who follows the teaching of Jesus Christ.

Church The organization which Christians belong to.

Civil war War between different groups of people who live in the same country.

Crusades Wars fought by Christians to remove the Turkish Muslims from the Holy Land.

Executed Put to death.

Famine A severe shortage of food.

Feudalism The system started by William I, where people had to obey and give services to their lord in return for land and protection.

Holy Land The land where Jesus lived and where biblical events took place.

House of Commons The lower chamber in the British Parliament.

Immoral Wrong behaviour.

Knights Men from noble families who served as soldiers.

Middle Ages The period of British history from 1066 to 1500, sometimes known as the medieval period.

Monks Men who follow a religious way of life, and live in a building called a monastery.

Muslims Followers of the religion of Islam, who believe in the teachings set out in the holy book, the Qur'an.

Norman Conquest The invasion and settlement of England by the Normans, after the Battle of Hastings in 1066.

Normandy A region of northern France.

Parliament In the Middle Ages this was a group of wealthy men who met to discuss how the country should be run and to make laws.

Parliamentary democracy The modern system of British government, where all laws and government decisions have to be agreed. Members of Parliament are chosen at elections.

Pilgrims People who make a journey to a holy place to pray.

Ransom The money demanded in return for the release of someone held prisoner.

Realm The area ruled by a king or queen.

Rebellion An uprising of people against their king or government .

Reform To try to make something better.

Regent Someone who rules in place of a very young king or queen.

Relics Religious objects, such as the remains of holy people.

Subjects The people of the country who obey their king.

Treachery Betrayal of friends or country.

Books to read

The Crusades by Peter Chrisp (Wayland, 1992)

The Kings and Queens of England and Scotland by Plantagenet Somerset Fry (Dorling Kindersley, 1990)

Life in the Middle Ages, Mark Ormrod (Wayland, 1991)

Medieval Realms by James Mason (Longman, 1991)

Norman Invaders and Settlers by Tony Triggs (Wayland, 1992)

Places to visit

Agincourt (*Azincourt* in French), Pas-de-Calais, Northern France
Tel: 21 04 41 12
You can tour the battlefield and visit a small museum.

Battle Abbey, near Hastings, East Sussex
Tel: 01424 773792
Site of the Battle of Hastings. Battle Abbey was founded by William the Conqueror.

Berkeley Castle, Berkeley, Gloucestershire
Tel: 01453 810332
12th Century castle where Edward II was murdered.

Bosworth Battlefield, Sutton Cheyney, Market Bosworth, Leicestershire
Tel: 01455 290429
Site of the battle where Richard III died fighting against the future Henry VII.

Caerphilly Castle, Mid Glamorgan, Wales
Tel: 01222 883143
One of the greatest surviving castles from medieval times.

Canterbury Cathedral, Canterbury, Kent
Tel: 01227 762862
Site of Thomas Becket's murder and the tomb of the Black Prince.

Tower of London, London
Tel: 0171 709 0765
Built by William I and the site of the imprisonment and murder of kings and princes.

Warwick Castle, Warwick, Warwickshire
Tel: 01926 495421
A fine medieval castle that was the home of the Earl of Warwick during the Wars of the Roses.

Westminster Abbey, Westminster, London
Tel: 0171 222 5152
Every coronation of a king and queen since 1066 has taken place here and many monarchs are also buried here. Geoffrey Chaucer, the first great English poet, was buried here in 1400.

Note: The language used in some of the quotations has been changed to make them easier to understand.

Index

Numbers in bold refer to pictures